Refined, Elegant Lady…

I0413430

Joyfully Balancing Living Alone With God,
and Socially Nurturing The Whole World;
Handing You Your Own Ticket to Soar!

Maryann Fenicato, Esq., Ph.D.

DEDICATION

This is for anyone who has always wanted, or who has otherwise been forced, to live or do things differently than the status quo, especially to live or do most things alone.

May this comfort, provide kudos, jump start, back you up, inspire, motivate, and/or lead you by personal example providing real life proof that even the most impossible dreams can come true.

Enjoy your Destiny!

.

CONTENTS

Acknowledgments

Chapters:

ACKNOWLEDGMENTS

Sincerest gratitude to my best friends Bobbie and Dave, Don, Ginger (and all of her wonderful friends), Tom, Kevin and everyone else who, like gifts from God, in any way inspire and/or encourage my seeming eccentricities and destined writing.

Rejoice and be glad, because when you least expect it, Karma will pay it back to you 10-fold!

Maryann Fenicato, Esq., Ph.D.

1
INTRODUCTION

WHAT is a refined, elegant lady?

WHERE would you find her?

And, what would she be DOING?

The answers may surprise you, free yourselves from old stereotypes. Why? For your own RECIPROCAL good, that is!

WHERE: Such a lady would not necessarily be a rare exception, living a rare life in the White House, or typically wearing expensive, cultured clothes bought at high-brow stores such as Talbots, let alone a "stuck-up" Southern Belle socialite dressed to the nines in uncomfortable layers with corsets and devilish shoes that hurt, etc., to properly and pretentiously attend a debutante ball! In fact, get this: She might be on the beach, yes even in a seemingly trash-party town like Key West, opting out of all the bad stuff, but basking in the good, especially the sun, thereby recharging her batteries for all the good she will do in a special way for others!

WHAT: It is a refined state of mind, an attitude, a humble yet higher spiritual level, priceless inner soul gold, an ideal to always aspire to, deserving and obtaining utmost respect! So, everyone should go for that "gold" in their own way, which shines out, and manifests beautifully. Respect others who do, or better yet, live it yourselves, I dare you--settle for nothing less, i.e., guys on your "arm," and ladies in your mirror, because ... you are worth it!

And, as to what she'd be DOING, instead of putting on airs and related things out in public, or cowering down to the status quo of being "married with children," she might just be living and doing most things alone with God, yes, even having dinner or travelling by herself! Yet, she might be even MORE social than the others, by writing her heart and soul out first indoors like a hermit, caring, altruistic, but then sharing it in many ways socially, finding a perfect balance to potentially qualitatively nurture the whole world!

So, the next time you see a lady doing something by herself, guess again, and instead of jumping to the wrong conclusions, treat her with the respect that she will immediately give you back, "Jack!"

This book will also show that it is nothing new, certainly not an alternative lifestyle or a road untaken. Rather, it is quite regular and RESPECTED, having been done since the beginning of time, and all over the world by so many others. The documented stats, facts, etc., that is, the PROOF, will be mind-boggling and eye-opening!

Most importantly, however, the main point is FREEDOM.

Unfortunately, many women have no choice but to live and do things alone, constantly regretting such a seemingly lonely fate, especially around holidays and Valentine's Day, of course. Many others waste their lives away, waiting at home for someone else to take them places, so they can be "seen" with them, avoid disapproving or dirty looks from others, etc. This book will free them in many ways, such as by showing them that others mainly do that to power-trip or because of jealousy. So, they must rescue themselves from such false beliefs, or remain a puppet on a string.

Moreover, this will show that many others have paved the way, such as Betty Friedan, who wrote a book called "The Feminine Mystique" long ago to rescue women who were married with children, socially correct yet MISERABLE! Although women can have their own careers now, the expectation has not changed, so their lives may be even more difficult, trying to juggle both a career and take care of a family. What they may not realize is that exactly because they could financially take care of themselves, they could live alone and have a larger, more quantitative world-wide family!

Believe it or not, this book will also help those who would NEVER adopt a similar lifestyle, by proving to them that a new attitude would be advantageous FOR THEM, as well, because they are unwittingly cutting THEMSELVES off from any reciprocal benefits, especially those not obvious, that would come their way.

Bottom Line: Freeing others frees YOURSELF!

2
HISTORY

This section will begin with my personal history to show how a young person who initially wanted to fit in, and certainly NOT have anything to do with pushy women's "lib" cause-rs, eventually changed her mind after she suddenly and surprisingly found herself suffering from the terrible stereotype assumed of female attorneys.

A. Personal

When I was young, I had **NO** interest in women's "lib," or "women's studies" later in college. That's because most who did seemed pushy and aggressive, as if they were venting (so if this book seems like it's venting, guess again). The truth is, back then, they seemed to be different, but just as bad as the historical oppression of women. It seemed to me they were just wasting their time, causing other problems which would only undermine their efforts, such as getting a bad name for themselves. Most importantly, I thought I could easily go with the flow, and find my niche in life, in a way that harmonized with others.

Why run against the wind, right?

In college, I also learned about people like Socrates and Marx, who followed their inner "daemon" both to their own benefit and detriment. A daemon is not an evil demon, rather, one's spirited soul, inner child, Divine destiny, etc., which might severely clash with the status quo, but like a moth to a flame, such people felt compelled to do that, even if it meant losing jobs, society's approval, and in extreme cases, even their own lives. At that time, that seemed silly or foolish, too.

Why not just find a way to fit in—right?

Later on, since I had only fit in to a few socially accepted roles, mainly: 1) excellent student and 2) meticulous, dependable, helpful paralegal, with a heart of gold, helping people get their American dream house, upon becoming an attorney, I thought I'd finally succeed. I went out of my way to fit the part, wearing dignified suits, moving to an apartment in a certain area, etc., but soon thereafter, I realized that I could never do everything that everyone expected, such as drive an appropriate car. Nor did I ever think my employers would expect me to go over to the "dark side," selling my soul by doing things unethically, just to win a case. They were surprised when I turned cases down, as well as the money that came with them, so then switched to trying to fool me by giving me cases with seemingly innocent victims, who turned out to be the bad guys. I was NOT going to help them get away with it!

The worst problem of all, however, was the way most people treated me as a female lawyer. The stereotype rhymes with "itch," and I found out the hard way, when it was too late, that many people really think you chose that career in the first place because you are like an attack dog or a pit bull, enjoying bloody fights. According to that pervasive stereotype, ladies are more evil, vindictive, vicious and victorious than men!

RESPECT for having the courage and smarts to pursue and secure such a difficult career was what I had expected, certainly NOT that!

So, during my last year of law school, I thought I would balance that out by finishing a separate doctorate degree in philosophy, but by then, the trend or tide had turned to deem it to be learning how to argue. That was the very opposite of why I leaned it and why I love it, especially the freedom it provides from imprisoning things like—stereotypes! Thus, at first, I taught it the way I learned it—aspiring to ethics and things with everlasting beauty such as virtues which make our lives wonderful, ideals that make it worth living, etc. But, eventually I evolved past even the things my professors had taught me, so after taking two entire years to think about it, I retied both professional careers "until further notice" and took a huge leap of faith into the unknown. Specifically, I obtained prior permission from a certain church, then moved to Key West to basically do a missionary "give back to God" one-year period.

However, despite all my efforts, which came on too strong for such a small town, and after teaching Philosophy for a semester at the local college and working two other jobs, but NEVER being appreciated for who I was and all that I could do for others, I mostly retreated into a hermit period. But, that's when I finally started enjoying my life, since I was free to focus on conducting continued personal research on all sorts of wonderful subjects. The awesome answers I found, which took everything I ever learned in school to a new level, made me rejoice, and warmed and freed my heart, mind and soul, so I'll share the priceless wealth with all of you now.

Ready?

Here goes:

B. World-Wide, Since the Beginning of Time

The Divine Feminine has been worshipped all over the globe since time began. Every culture had one or more female goddesses, which were held in HIGHER esteem than men because they contained the secret of creation. Although they couldn't do it without men, who provided the spark, men couldn't bring it to life, or into this world. So, women were worshipped for more than just baby making—they were seen as the portal between this and the world beyond, the magic crossover point or connection. And, since human babies require more nurturing for longer periods than other species, they were essential to not only their offspring's growth, but extremely necessary for their entire tribe's survival!

However, since males are generally physically stronger, they sought domination, so patriarchal societies developed especially because of Christianity. All kinds of evidence is now available that proves how it was used and abused to make men superior, especially priests, as if we need them as intermediaries or educators. In fact, above and beyond pretend, and pretext witch hunts, even Christ was killed, so they could subjugate and relegate women to inferiority, and use the Bible as an excuse. That was purposefully done by severely editing the gospels, leaving some out entirely, etc.

Today, more and more sources of proof are coming out of hiding, bravely revealing and restoring the truth.

Yet back then, since the Divine Feminine had ruled majestically for so long, it had been time for the opposite to prevail, and the souls of all humankind to learn lessons from doing things that way, too. So, Divine, universal and/or cosmic forces did not step in to stop that, because humankind was given free will to choose its fate.

Instead, She reasserted herself peacefully from behind the scenes, operating slowly and steadily via higher consciousness ever since. Specifically, it inspired various obvious women's movements, and has worked more subtly, poignantly and effectively thru the arts.

1. The Arts: Entertaining yet Educating

Countless examples could be cited as to how the arts have slowly reconstructed the scope of all that a woman could and, in fact, should be, not just for themselves, but to benefit all humankind.

The well-known Scarlet O'Hara movie character took matters into her own hands and saved Tara, her land, in "Gone With the Wind," providing quite a role model, even for high society women. In a perhaps lesser-known television program called, "Remington Steele," which catapulted its male character, Pierce Brosnan, to become the next James Bond, a female private investigator created a fictitious male boss to appease clients who wouldn't have hired a woman, despite her track record.

But, instead of providing a long list of examples here, which would include all sorts of media, not limited to books, movies, television, etc., let's look at certain monumental women's movements.

2. Women's Suffrage

The first women's movement concerned suffrage, the right to vote. One can only imagine how hard it must have been to start the ball rolling, and more importantly, how nasty the opposition must have been, especially from OTHER women! So, those pioneers deserve our respect, especially for the following reason, something that many of you might not know, so get ready for an eye-opener:

3. Legal Chattel, Like Cattle!

Women used to be considered "chattel," like cattle, literally, personal property possessed only by men, not themselves, so they certainly could not own anything. The system was stacked against them, making it impossible for them to hold their own, and therefore, entirely dependent on men. Real or personal property, such as land, titles, etc., could only be owned by males, and sold, conveyed, passed on, etc. to other males, which is why it was so important for families to have a son, especially for royalty.

4. Betty Friedan's "Feminine Mystique"

The next major revolution, or wave of feminism that rocked the world was created by nothing but a book (like this, hint, hint!) entitled, "The Feminine Mystique," written by Betty Friedan during the 1960's. Betty had gone to a school reunion only to find that most of her female classmates, specifically those who were, of course, socially correctly "married with children," and even those who had it all financially, were NOT happy. In fact, some were miserable, especially after their children left the "nest."

So, she put together a book by interviewing many of them, conducting lots of research, etc., to save, rescue and lead women out of such seemingly nice, but buried-alive prisons. She proved that the "married with children" stereotype, the "feminine mystique" that expects women to be fulfilled by such a limited life, was NOT enough. In a word, her solution was "education."

5. Careers Can Make Life More Difficult

During the years that followed, many women certainly got educated, and stopped being mere stay-at-home Moms. Having a career outside the home provided many things, including more money, intellectual challenges and self-esteem, but juggling or balancing that with childcare and other home responsibilities can be very difficult and burdensome. So, today, some women actually pay other women to take care of their children, choosing the money, prestige, power, etc. of a career over them, supposedly for their benefit, of course. In so doing, however, they willingly sacrifice quality time, and the once-in-a-lifetime opportunity to bond, nurture and personally enhance their growth. Especially later on, they might have enjoyably reaped what they sowed.

The problem is that despite women's current ability to have careers, the "married with children" stereotypical social status quo expectation, which is the same as the "feminine mystique," has NOT changed. Most people still think it is required, regardless.

6. Beware of Reverse Roles

Today, many women have more lucrative and impressive careers than men. Relationships and families wherein women "wear the pants," however, can be very problematic, especially for their children. Like children of abusive parents, but for different reasons, they are confused and must run against the wind from the beginning. Most of the time, fighting at home turns them against the reverse roles, so many act out by getting in trouble with the law. Even the submissive husbands can regret it in many ways, becoming sick because they can't even voice, let alone control, things, and their emotions or even their careers may suffer every time their lady "wins another one for the team," as they say. After witnessing this myself in many ways, relegating men to such lower roles, such as "Mr. Mom" obviously may not be the answer, either.

7. Women Living Alone, Supporting Themselves

The "married with children" social stereotype has created other problems, such as an astronomical world population, which rapidly depletes the earth's resources, especially those like natural gas, that just can't be easily or readily replaced, if at all. In Asian countries, pollution, lack of building space, etc., has prompted people to build and live in skyscrapers, high up where they can get fresh air!

So, as engineers, scientists and all sorts of other experts try to figure all the related world issues out, and since the right to have children is inalienable, here's a much easier solution. Instead of being mistreated as something wrong or weird, the following should be seen, deemed, treated, and most importantly, **RESPECTED** as a NICE, CORRECT choice or OPTION for

SOME, certainly not required for all, because it would in turn, BENEFIT the whole WORLD:

> **The stereotype could simply be changed, this time finally, once and for all, allowing women who'd want to, especially those who could support themselves, to do most things and live happily ALONE.**

Duh!

3
CONFLICTING STEREOTYPES
AND INNER CHILDREN

The following conflicting male and female stereotypes are presented to prove how wrong it is to expect a lady not to live alone or to be able to take care of herself at all. Yet, on the other hand, she is regardless expected and even required to fully care for her physical children, but not, however, her Divine inner child!

A. Under the Stetson

Notice how socially correct or commendable it is for a male to be a "lone ranger," showing up, helping others, and leaving before anyone notices or gets any chance to thank them. Lonesome cowboys are romantic and the unfettered lifestyle of the "Marlboro man" was so appealing that it easily sold lots of cigarettes. Today, such mysterious older men, especially high plain drifters, are of a new younger breed, especially dangerous teenage vampires, right? Their allure is even more desirable.

B. Male Superheroes

Also notice that most male superhero role models live, work or spend most of their time alone. Same for similar folk heroes like Zorro and Robin Hood, who provide admirable vigilante justice.

C. Female Stereotypes

Unlike the above, a woman who can take care of herself, mostly comes across as a "bad ass" or a word that rhymes with "itch." Such stereotypes are even more likely if she works in certain professions, especially any kind of law enforcement, let alone a lawyer. Instead of respect, she is feared, but most of it only covers up others' jealousy, but the truth is easily seen, regardless.

We need to get behind the stereotype to get rid of it. It is founded on the idea that a woman can't take care of herself, and shouldn't even try, but notice how quickly that changes if she is taking care of and/or protecting her own children—oh, that's the best thing of all, right? So, if we deconstruct or break that down, notice how false it really is—she can't take care of herself, and shouldn't, but can and must care for and protect her children, something that is actually much harder to do!

And, more importantly, what about her own inner child?

D. Inner Children

Some women are simply called to different destinies than the status quo. At first, they may fight such a destiny, really only fighting themselves, an internal battle, wanting to easily fit in with others, instead. But, if they are meant to be different, their inner child will not let them, because even if repressed, it will never die, rather, some back to haunt them until they step up and attain their destiny.

So, such women may wind up having no choice at all but to be different from others, because even when they really try to fit in, they may feel, for instance, cursed. It is not, of course, really a curse, rather, their inner child, which they can and should have taken care of all these years, but repressed it for sake of others. It simply wants and deserves the same treatment as other children!

Yet, an inner child is even more important than physical children, because if allowed to fully grow into self-actualization of the Divine, instead of just a few lives, it can help many others. So, as a specific example, a lady could instead chose to create books, not children…

4
CREATING BOOKS,
NOT CHILDREN

This chapter will explain why a life dedicated to the creation of something good for many others, not just a few personal children, such as educational, enlightening, inspiring and freeing books, should be RESPECTED. Even the best or "Good Book," itself, the Bible, of course, does not mandate marriage and/or children!

A. No Commandment!

Gee, the Ten Commandments just don't include any requiring children or marriage, now do they—eh?

Did God make a mistake?

Did Moses edit one out?

I really don't think so, but you decide for yourself. Why? Plain common sense dictates that if either was so important, it would have been not only included, but placed up high, right under the first one, top dog, top shelf!

Yet, what's even more surprising is that the men who severely edited the Bible to their advantage did not add one, either. Why? Because obviously, one of the best ways to tie a woman down is to keep her chained to, and very busy taking care of, a husband and lots of children!

B. Other Good Books

Gee, there are other good books besides the Bible (or even this one—right? Ha!) One of the very best on this particular issue is Plato's "Symposium." The entire book is surprisingly good reading, because instead of boring subjects, it is one big thorough discussion about love, with many speakers addressing different aspects. After all the others put in their two cents, which are everything from heart-warming to entertaining, Socrates explains the truth, and he does it via something very unusual for his era—he quotes and gives respectful credit to a lady, Diotima, for teaching him this, herein summarized short and sweet:

To outlive their own lives, that is, leave a lasting legacy, people basically chose between one or two options. Most chose to have children, while others opt to create other things, such as books.

C. Quality and Quantity

Looking with eyes of truth, one can easily see that writing many books that could help many other people creates something else, quantity, so the seeming quality of taking care of a few physical children gets spread out, and placed on a higher, selfless, spiritual level. So, seen correctly, that perfectly balances the typical choice of taking care of only a few significant others. Yet, its potential far exceeds that, making much more possible, even world-round.

D. Rock Your World

Most writers, however, are not out to rock or change the world. They have something inside, a passion, that has to get out, period. If they make money, great, but if not, they'd not only do it anyway, but HAVE TO, because otherwise, it would churn and burn inside, and turn into something really negative such as spine pain that could undermine their whole lives. I personally felt cursed until I began writing books on these spiritual subjects.

Why? Because most writers were "rocked" by one good book or more, themselves, so they may feel the need to reciprocate. Some entertain, but others go as far as to help others, because even if they would only wind up helping one person, that would still be ok, because they, themselves WERE that person!

E. Hiding Out While Writing is NORMAL!

It is well-known, understood, and even expected for a writer to write inside, as if hiding out from the world on purpose. Most need some sort of microcosm, a special spot, an out of the way alcove, etc. Notice how similar that is to an artist who might need a "studio" that itself sparks creativity, a musician might need a garage or sound studio to get them in the mood, a computer genius might need to work in a dark "cave," and even business people might need a "think tank," etc. So, getting away from others to create mostly all by oneself is NORMAL, respected and expected for the various arts and even writers. Therefore, notice how silly it would be for anyone to treat a lady writer, who spends so much time writing inside anyway, differently if she lived alone as well.

Duh!

Get this, too: How much time would ANY writer even have for anyone else who did live with them? See how unfair that would be to them?

F. Keeping to Themselves While Out in Public

Writers are also very likely to keep to themselves while out in public, anyway.

> **They have FAR MORE MEANINGFUL, and QUALITATIVE social interaction THROUGH their books on a higher spiritual level, so they may have less need to go out and socialize in the first place!**

And, when they do, they may still be thinking about something they want to write, and an idea can hit at any time, so they are well-known for writing on napkins at restaurants. Notice how NORMAL that is.

1. Restaurants

So, if a female writer went to a restaurant by herself, why should that be deemed wrong in any way? She could very well be doing that for many good reasons, such as getting something to eat to survive because she wrote so much she didn't even have time to go to the grocery store. Gee, her motives might NOT be the stereotypical hoping to "meet someone," especially the people who work at any particular place. In fact, such a writer may go to many restaurants all over town, so no particular wait staff person, manager, etc., should get any ideas!

The situation gets worse if she is pretty—people may assume she is a call-girl, escort, etc.

> **And, more importantly, if they "hit on her" and she gets mad or insulted because she is a refined, elegant lady that deserves to be treated with RESPECT, NOT "hey, baby, how you 'doin?," guys will try to save face by acting like she "ain't all that," and should somehow appreciate such a low-level compliment. Amazing!**

Other women who are jealous because they never get "hit on," could side with the men, so the situation could get silly or stupid.

Yet, most of the time, the people who have a problem seeing a pretty lady out on their own are either afraid that their guy might notice her, etc., or be jealous in many ways, wishing she were free to do things herself.

So, what everyone should realize is that writers need soul food, and many get that by eating alone, because it is the perfect blend of "alone time" to think, with some limited social interaction. So, they might really want to keep it that way, even if they are women!

Even more importantly, notice that is NOT someone who is foolishly "TREATING themselves." Instead, they may be "banking" it, using it to work very hard inside their own heads, and then pay it forward to help others.

2. Travelling

The same would be true if a writer were travelling. The travelling itself may not be done for fun, or even be their choice at all.

And, when they do, their minds might be "travelling" even more inside their heads, thinking about all sorts of things to write about. So, again, seeing a person, especially a female, travel alone is not a cause for alarm or wrong assumptions. In fact, some run-aways are actually smart and courageous for doing so! But, no one should jump to any conclusions, because if it was their choice, most writers would much rather be in peaceful proximity of writing instruments, so they can properly take care of ideas when they hit.

Moreover, although travelling can be fun sometimes, most writers are introverts, so despite the fun, most can't wait to get back.

G. Balancing Social Sales, Appearances, etc.

It is also quite NORMAL, expected and respected for any artist, especially writers, to shy away from the more public aspects of their craft, those necessary yet burdensome, such as sales and marketing. Some might not mind making personal appearances, such as book signings, because there they may receive kudos.

Society does already understand that they would not want to have anything to do with the nitty-gritty pavement-pounding, even if it is done these days online via social media and networks.

Since finding the right balance of time, delegation, etc., could be difficult, at least others understand. So, why not extend that understanding to encompass the rest of a writer's life, as well?

H. Home Alone

There are only so many hours in a day, and writers might have to do many other related things "home alone" as well, such as preliminary or continued research. More spiritual subjects might require time to conduct meditation, whereas more difficult subjects such as abuse may take up even more time, etc.

Again, how fair would that be to anyone else living with them?

I. Doing Others a Favor

So, for all the above-mentioned reasons, a person might chose to create something besides physical children as a legacy. Notice that in so doing, because the amount of time required to do so many other related things, the truth is this:

> By voluntarily choosing to live alone, they might be doing others who might want to live with them a very selfless, benevolent:
>
> **FAVOR!**

J. Selfless Favor ... Respected!

Such a SELFLESS favor should, therefore, not be considered wrong or weird, but be appreciated, venerated and RESPECTED!

K. Respect is a Karmic Reciprocal Mirror

Instead of immediately jumping to wrong assumptions, conclusions or stereotypes, when a person respects someone else first, giving them the benefit of the doubt, like presuming them innocent until proven guilty, a karmic reciprocal relationship is created, as well. Like looking in a mirror, it looks back at you, and boomerangs back, sometimes big-time!

More importantly, why assume the worst and cut YOURSEVLES off from all the benefits that a person who chooses to create great things besides children might provide? And, most importantly, of all, **NEVER assume that the only thing such a person could reciprocate is a mere book!**

Karma is a powerful force that defies mortal understanding. Operating perhaps on a quantum physics level, most people would agree that even the smallest kindness could be paid back to you 10-fold. So, when you treat such a person with kindness and respect, especially one who might be nurturing the whole world silently from behinds the scenes., you may not merely obtain their reciprocity, rather receive something much bigger from that a mysterious force, itself, which has no limit.

Understanding the true potential power and extent of all that, would anyone willingly cut themselves off?

Duh!

RESPECT is the ANSWER!

5
AMAZING LEGAL MATTERS

Unlike all the benevolent things discussed herein thus far, this section will explain how the law has CHANGED accordingly, to prove why being "married with children" might be a big mistake.

A. Before the Change

In olden times, as already mentioned above, women were nothing but chattel, a personal possession like cattle, of men. Since they could not own anything, and before they could have personal careers, they could certainly not support themselves.

B. Finding Fault

Back then, hardly anyone got divorced for various reasons. First and foremost, it was considered a social scandal or scar, a "pox" one would put on one's whole family, something all would have to regret and "live down." The few that did get divorced had to find fault, namely, had to find proof that would fit under the old legal "fault grounds," which was very difficult. Here's why:

Women who were miserable pretended to stay married for the sake of their children, but the truth is that some could have handled the social scar but not the financial responsibility. Men remained married mostly because they would have had to sacrifice significant amounts of money or property, such as pay substantial amounts of alimony and/or child support to women who had no other source of income, etc. Those were the days when a woman could easily get "half," but it just wasn't "worth it" for either side.

C. No Fault

Once women significantly joined the workforce, things changed and so did the law. Since they had income, they didn't need "half" as before. Some could even support themselves, perhaps even making more money than men. So, it would have been unfair to men if the law did not change.

Yet, the law changed in other ways, as well. To prevent either party, but mostly women, from being stuck in a marriage, especially to abusers, who knew the rules and easily avoided getting caught with enough proof to fit the old fault grounds, a new category was created, known as "No Fault." The new rules enable people to get out of marriages in various other ways, much quicker if both parties agree, by simply claiming "irreconcilable differences," etc. But, even if they don't, a marriage can basically be deemed done after a two-year separation period, so one party can just leave and get their way ("get 'er done") regardless, from a safe distance afar.

D. Downright Dirty Durations, etc.

Despite the new laws, things can still be downright dirty. Far beyond unfair or cutthroat, cases can be made to linger on for amazing durations, etc. Why? To get what they want, their way, especially to hurt the other party as much as possible, making them "pay" financially and emotionally, some people will resort to terrible things, especially those who know the system and the specific things that will trigger it. Not everyone will want out peacefully; some will want revenge lasting as long as possible.

I went through a divorce myself, and it was certainly one of the scariest things I ever experienced to watch the person I trusted enough to marry and share things that I never told anyone else, do a "Dr. Jekyll and Mr. Hyde." Squaring off with a stranger, or even another educated attorney is one thing, but going up against someone like that who went over to the dark side, and will use everything, and I do mean everything, they know against you, is something else. It made a nice, peaceful paralegal like me who had always mostly helped people with the peaceful paperwork required to get their American dream home, suddenly go to law school for rotection!

Luckily, one of my professors, a Dean, listened to my situation and advised me the truth for free in an academic setting. He counseled me to not even try to prevent the divorce because it would be too much of an emotional and financial strain. Rather, it would be better to simply wait for the two-year no-fault period to run out, and focus instead on bettering my life through law school. I'm so glad and grateful for that sage advice, that I've always felt a duty to pay it forward. So, I've enjoyed providing free academic advice to others ever since.

During law school, I also interned with a family law judge. There, I unfortunately witnessed and learned so many despicable things, that I decided never to become a divorce attorney, or marry again. But, instead of mentioning any specifics here, I'll refer you to an amazingly thorough example of how far people would go, even to the extent of destroying another person's life, just to get what they want, in another book called, "The Art of Racing in the Rain," by Garth Stein. It is a "good read" regardless, containing something for just about everyone, written in a very eye-opining way, as if by a dog, but also containing macho "guy stuff" about professional car racing, and a surprise ending. All the enjoyable stuff balances out the terrible divorce—you'll see what I mean.

E. Male "Gold Diggers" and "Mr. Moms"

Worst of all, the new laws enable men to become "gold diggers," or "Mr. Mom's." Some of them see it as their turn, since so many women have dug gold out of men. But, the new twist is that many women make more than men, and even if they do not, they could be deemed able, so they could be forced to work a miserable job, and only to pay their husbands to stay at home and be Mr. Mom!

F. Avoidance is Very SMART!

So, someone like me who never really meant to, but obtained two separate doctorate degrees and three others to balance terrible child abuse, could be a freelance writer, nurturing so many others while working at home. I could do that instead of working a miserable professional job in an air-conditioned office that would escalate my spine problems, force me to live up north in the terrible cold outside, as well, near my Mom, etc. But, if I were dumb enough to get married again, I may have to do the opposite, and suffer all sorts of other pain while PAYING for it, in more ways than one.

Duh!

Thus, my life is just one example of why avoiding all that is NOT wrong or weird, but, in fact, very SMART!

G. Marriage Misery

Most parents want their kids to get married. But, if they do it the wrong way or for wrong reasons, it can backfire, and they can actually get the very opposite of what they want. Although they'd never admit it, they'd have no one but themselves to blame.

Many marriages are miserable!

Even if people didn't get what they wanted, expected, or even deserves, many stay together, and make their kids miserable, too.

Duh!

Yet, they still expect their kids to get married, regardless, supposedly for their own good, while their real reasons can be very selfish. They want to appear socially correct themselves, avoid illegitimate children, elopements, etc. And afterward, no matter what happens, they expect their kids to stay married, even if they are just as miserable. So, the situation can become a catch-22 that can continue longer than even a terrible court case, namely, for GENERATIONS until someone finally has enough guts to stop.

In front of others, or at first, parents or spouses pretend to care, but eventually life can become a prison, tied like a ball and chain first to parents who do not really care about your feelings at all, and can't wait to pass your responsibility on to your spouse, who could simply do the same for the entire rest of your life.

One could want out so bad, only to wind up jumping from one "frying pan into the fire." Love can be fake and false, based on nothing but lies, and used against you. Before you know it, both parents and spouses can join together and try to kill your dreams and chain you to a life of sheer misery.

Accordingly, marriage could be nothing but misery!

H. The Ultimate Test

They say hindsight is 20-20 vision, so here's an easy eye-opener.

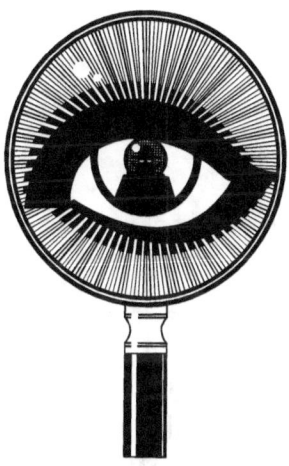

This test removes blinders, false belief mandated by others, or even seemingly sweet rose-colored glasses, revealing the truth, so each of you can figure out what's really worth it, not for them, but for you.

Ready?

> **Take any relationship that you currently have now, or have had in the past, either with people or animals, and look back. Notice how much of the time you were actually happy, and compare it to how much you were not.**
>
> **Was/is it worth it?**

You decide—you be your own judge and jury. I dare you. You

only have one life, and the only person living or wasting it is you.

See?

I. Avoiding Repetition

Seeing the above is believing, and another way it can help all of you is to avoid repeating the same relationships over and over again.

J. Legal Disclaimer

The ONLY change that this book zealously advises, for everyone's own good, is:

> **A change of ATTITUDE regarding women who live or do most things alone--give them the RESPECT that they (and you, in turn) deserve!**

It will boomerang back to each of you in many ways, perhaps even from karma, with 10-fold force.

This book does NOT advise anyone to adopt such a lifestyle, and certainly does not advise making any drastic changes that you might really regret, such as ending various relationships abruptly.

If various things learned herein, especially the eye-openers, lead any of you to do so, then enjoy being the master and commander of your lives, making such decisions for yourself, by yourself.

Yet, notice how readily all of this could help others.

Instead of finding fault, apply "no fault" here, too, right?--and enjoy.

6
BEING DIFFERENT MAY <u>NOT</u> BE A CHOICE OR ALWAYS FUN!

When people see me doing something different, they immediately assume I am doing something wrong and should be given dirty looks or even stopped especially if I seem to be enjoying it. But, the truth is that many of us have no choice, and it is not always fun, something no fun at all, because others do not understand. So, this chapter will provide substantive explanation.

Let's start with behavior we all observe of others from time to time, which may seem bad.

Many people do unusual things do get attention, such as put bright blue color streaks in their hair. When I see something like that, I do not immediately jump to the wrong conclusions like most people—that they are wrong or weird. Nor am I naive, the opposite extreme, rather, I simply give them the benefit of the doubt until I find out more.

Yes, it may seem they are being deviant now, doing things that will get them the wrong kind of attention, or even a bad reputation, but I know from personal experience and all the students I have taught, especially, that:

> MOST TRY VERY HARD TO FIT IN FIRST—IT IS ONLY AFTER WE SEE THAT NO MATTER WHAT WE DO, IT WILL NOT WORK, THAT WE TURN TO DIFFERENT THINGS.

In fact, many are super-sensitive, easily hurt, so they may snap at you for protection, to avoid getting hurt by you. So, if you back off and treat then nice, you may uncover a heart of gold.

For instance, I remember working with a guy who was so mean people called him the "troll." He supervised the copy room within a corporation. No one even bothered to try to get him fired because they assumed he "knew someone," otherwise, he would have been eliminated long ago. As for me, I really enjoyed having the excuse to go there, and maybe even hang out a while, because I had my eye on another guy who's office was close by. So, I had an extra reason to try to at least be friends. Eventually, he admitted to me that the reason he was mean was to stop people from being mean to him, which was very likely to happen because of his appearance, the kind that engendered jokes. Befriending him wound up working out for many other people as well, because I was soon asked by many others to take copy jobs to him so they could avoid him, giving me extra reasons to go and hang out there. How about that--a win-win-win for everyone!

I also recall a student of mine who purposefully caused attention to himself by sitting the first day of class, not in a chair, but on a window sill. Since the weather was very warm, all the windows were open, so he sat cross-legged Indian-style, as if in a lotus meditation pose, with one leg or bent knee, hanging out the window. I didn't see him until I took roll, and when I looked up, he smiled, but gave me one of those looks that I know all too well, as if ready for a confrontation or showdown which he was going to enjoy, a show or spectacle put on in front of the rest of the class. He thought he'd upset me, but I surprised him by stating the truth, that if I was in his place and not wearing a dress, I'd certainly do such a smart thing, too. I got a laugh from the rest of the class, and NOT one that hurt his feelings. Soon thereafter, when I least expected it, he voluntarily came down and sat in a regular chair.

Blue hair also seems to be big a tip-off. Male or female, young or old, wearers want attention. If you buck them, it'll blow up in your face, but if you befriend them, you may be amazed.

The reason this works, however, is because they can tell I am not simply pacifying or schmoozing them, trying to avoid a problem. I actually understand and don't blame them. Although I certainly never go as far as to condone any of it, I certainly provide caring.

Early on, many of us are put in impossible situations, by our parents, peers, etc. At first, we try and try to make everyone happy, but soon we may realize that some people are so miserable that they will never be happy no matter what we do, so there is no reason to waste time trying. And, if their expectations conflict with the rest of society, we may have a second set of impossibilities. As if that were not enough, what you do to keep certain people at bay can conflict with the rest of society, so you get burned like a candle on both ends, and a person can only take so much of that. Living like a "man without a country" gets tiresome, that is, never having any rest or emotional support, so at some point, we up and decide that we are going to go against one set whether they like it or not.

We are not being head—strong or bad kids. We are not like wild horses that have to be tamed. We deserve respect.

Later on in life, after we have changed in many ways, we may give it another shot, but:

> SOME OF US WERE DESTINED
> TO BE DIFFERENT THAN OTHERS,
> WHETHER **WE** LIKE IT OR NOT!

At some point we may even fight ourselves, internally conflicted, which is not worth it. **We eventually realize have to be different so as not to lose ourselves, so we have no real choice.**

Get this: It would actually be "easier" to just adopt one of the other alternative lifestyles, such as gay, lesbian, bisexuals, sex change surgery or transvestites, etc., to fit into pre-existing categories, for which there is some support. But, someone like me who ONLY wants a slight change from normal, just to live and do most things alone, even in a place like Key West, where it may seem people are so open minded that they'd accept just about anything, the truth is that's like running against the wind, because it doesn't fit into any accepted alternative category others understand.

People don't get this. Hence, this book! After this, they will.

7
HERMITS, MONKS, WISE SAINTS AND SOLITARIES: RESPECTED WORLD-ROUND SINCE TIME BEGAN

Again , since the beginning odd time, all around the world, people have gone off to live alone. Some even went far away, to difficult deserts or islands in dangerous locations that can only be accessed at certain times of the year, such as Skellig Michael in Ireland. The annals of history are full of such people, who went beyond the typical lives of monks, priests or nuns, who lived inside church rectories with other priests or convents with other nuns.

A. Venerated and Respected

They lived completely alone, and they were actually VENERATED and RESPECTED for being more pious than the rest!

B. Wise Advice

Most were also sought out for WISE ADVICE. How about that!

C. Fashionable

Here's interesting history: During a certain era in England, it was actually fashionable and smart for rich people to "have one," as if a pet. Yet, better than butlers or other servants who were paid, they worked for nothing, taking care of various aspects of the house, grounds, etc., in exchange for a place to live. And, they would do the tasks far better and be much more trustworthy, since they were living and doing things for God, not for pay.

I, myself, have done things similarly the entire time that I have lived in Key West. I've done light maintenance, yard work, caretaking of grounds, plants trees, etc., I've even been entrusted with the keys to the rest of the residences, even to portions that I never occupy, to keeping an eye on everything. Especially outside,

I take pride in making things look very nice, even if only for the benefit of tourists passing by.

Yet, that really benefits the entire island. Here's why: If we all did out part, even if limited to our particular spot, it would really be a beautiful paradise, heaven on earth.

Back to historical hermits, etc.:

D. Sacrificing Wealth for a Simple Life

Throughout most of earth's history, people understood and appreciated those that gave up a traditional family life a solitary one. People were venerated for sacrificing wealth for a simple life. They were not deemed weird or wrong, rather, wise, venerable saints to be RESPECTED.

The same respect should be given even to someone doing that, even if they are smart enough to live on a beautiful island. NOT everyone does that because they are a lazy "beach-bum" who "doesn't want to work." Give everyone a chance before you judge, even if it seems like everyone else came to do that—so what!

E. Helping Others

Moreover, hermits were respected although many of them hardly ever did anything for any other person, at all. If sought out by someone for wise council, they would not encourage it, rather, treat as an inconvenience that interrupted their solitude. So, a person who writes many books to help others in so many ways should be **all the MORE respected!**

F. Jesus, Himself

Most importantly, notice that JESUS himself became a solitary when others would have sought other's help. For forty days and forty nights, the devil tempted Him, but instead of calling in a cavalry of angels, etc., he undertook it all alone. So, He is perhaps the very best example of that, as well!

8

OTHER STEREOTYPES

A. Nice, Good Categories—Why Not Assume That?

Taking this one step further, this book is not just about the RESPECT with which a refined, elegant lady should be treated. Rather, the bigger picture or goal is to address the immediate, widespread practice of dropping people in bad categories, assuming wrong stereotypes, etc.

Why don't pick good, nice ones, instead?

Duh!

Believe it or not, I see this in Key West more than anywhere else. Here, things are supposed to be the opposite, that is, everyone is supposed to come here to do bad "trash-party" things, especially smoking, drinking, "sex, drugs, rock and roll." So, if you did not, you're wrong—how about that?

But, just as surprising is the fact that you can't really do what you want. When you visit, it may seem that everyone is so very nice, understanding and open-minded that anyone could come here and be their real selves, no matter what that means. But, it is still a small town, so although it has very unusual categories, perhaps more than most places, you still have to fit into one that they can understand, or else you'll be mistreated.

For instance, I love to go to open houses on Sunday afternoons. Since I am not in a position to actually buy any, I've explained to most realtors that I don't want to sit around waiting until I am, rather, scope things out it in the meantime, which is smart. Although most are nice, they never really seemed to get it, until one day, someone came up with an acceptable category for me, which is: "pre-view." That got around, so now I'm given understanding looks. That could have happened long-before, but gee, I did not have the magic password. So glad I fit in now!

B. Sicilian Truths

1. NOT Bragging About "Knowing Someone"

Another particular stereotype I would like to address concerns being of Sicilian descent, in my case, 100%. Here in Key West, people think I mention that to make them fear me (horse head in bed, etc.), as if I am bragging about mafia connections, etc. How silly! That's because here in "Bubba-ville," "Conchs" born here constantly feel the need to drop hints about "who they know," so they WRONGLY ASSUME I'm doing that, too. How stupid!

I mention it for two other good reasons, and I have a nice surprise. So, read on:

2. Great Laugh

First, where I am from, which is Pittsburgh, the place is so ethnic that even attorney's typically use such fun, jovial material as ice-breaker jokes to begin speeches, classes, etc. Why? It's SMART because it is almost guaranteed to get a laugh. I remember one saying that his wife is only "one-quarter" Sicilian, and luckily so…, and he never even got to finish his sentence because the whole room erupted in laughter. Why? Because it is common knowledge that Sicilian women can be especially hard to handle.

Notice how humble and honest it is for me to mention that.

Yet, we can be worth knowing for other reasons.

3. Street Smart

Another reason I mention it is because I am a refined, elegant lady who lives and does most things alone in Key West, so for my protection, I must convey the concept that I am NOT a push-over. Nor am I here for any bad trash-party reasons. No, Sicilians are street-smart, wiser and less gullible than most, so I'm advising others, for their own benefit, to skip even trying to take advantage! To put it another way, there is no reason to even get to a point where a "horse's head" is needed--why even "go there." Why not just do nice things for others, such as not judge them wrongly!

4.   More Emotional Empathy and Understanding

Our street smarts, however, extend to understanding people's deeper inner/emotional needs more and perhaps better than others. That's why we can be great life coaches, motivators, etc.

So, for instance, if a hair "butcher" hacked your hair mercilessly, cutting off over 7 inches and ruining it in so many other ways that it took 2 years to get it right again, and you cried for months, let alone the total duration, others may not understand the depth of the internal damage, but we might. Something like that can have a detrimental domino effect, wrecking not just "dead hair" that "grows back" but a person's whole life. No, it would NOT be silly to be very upset, especially if the other person did it on purpose. In fact, even under such extremely evil circumstances, instead of "horse's head" personal revenge, we may advise letting karma's mysterious force take care of it, because no one can run from that!

5.   Sweet Surprise

Yet, I also have a surprise:

> The biggest reason why we Sicilians are really worth having as friends is that if you do good by us, we can be just as passionate and "deadly" about treating you even BETTER than you did us! So, we can be the very best friends to have because if we think we owe you, we think it's "big time," and we will ENJOY going the extra mile, certainly not abandoning you in a time of need, or be a false friend, etc.   In fact, we can be SWEETER than the rest—so, go ahead, just give us a reason to prove it---I dare you!

C. NOT Pretending!

Yet, the stereotype that needs to be stopped perhaps most of all is:

> The **WRONG ASSUMPTION** that any woman who lives or does most things alone is just **PRETENDING** to prefer that, but really wishing she could be with someone or even married-with-children!
>
> Since that speaks for itself, enough said!

9
RESPECT YOURSELF!

I remember a country song lyric, saying, "I like my women a little on the trashy side." That seemed fun when I was younger, but if you live with a snake, one of these days, you'll get bit. In fact, many people who seek out cutthroat attorneys regret it, because they can turn and burn, getting what they paid for themselves.

So, settling for nothing less than a refined, elegant lady as a friend, on your "arm" if male, or in your own mirror, can be a really good idea, because you reap what you sow. Men, as yourselves if you'd you really want a trashy person to be the mother of your children, or otherwise "haunt" you, perhaps for the rest of your life?

In a word, if you RESPECT yourself enough to require that, in another word, you will benefit YOURSELF.

RESPECT YOURSELF!

10
HAND IT TO 'EM!

Now let's have some real fun!

The biggest reason I wrote this book is for you and I to have something that can be handed to others, put right under their faces or noses. To make it even more obvious and easy, highlight or tab any special sentence, paragraph, or section.

This is especially meant to RESCUE any lady who thinks she must wait at home, wasting her life like a controlled puppet on a string until someone arrives to go out with her. GO OUT, and do things YOURSELF, even restaurants and travelling and:

USE THIS AS AN EXCUSE!

SEE THIS AS YOUR TICKET to ride, to reach the stars and become one yourself, your Divine destiny. Don't let anyone hold you back. Fly, soar, and enjoy, and remember, you're not just doing it for yourself, but to free the rest in the world, as well!

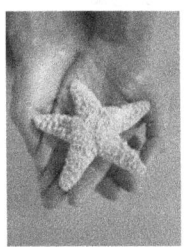

ABOUT THE AUTHOR

Maryann Fenicato, Esq., Ph.D. was born in Pittsburgh, PA, USA. From highly-accredited Duquesne University, she earned 2 separate doctorates in Law and Philosophy (Ethics), and 3 other degrees.

<u>Currently</u>: She is a fun, charismatic, motivational, inspirational and educational speaker, teacher, guru, mentor and life coach, who travels domestically and abroad to speak in front of large groups at universities, colleges and other educational institutions, churches, youth facilities and other spiritual organizations, businesses and corporations. Yet, she also enjoys privately counselling individuals confidentially, especially troubled teens or adults who have yet to maximize their destined potential, inspiring them to step up and free themselves to live the life they were meant to live. A prolific author who's already accomplished an amazingly multi-faceted destiny, living the life she's always dreamed of in beautiful Key West, she enjoys sharing and showing others how to do it, too. For any such engagements, contact: **mafenicato@hotmail.com**
See website: **maryannfenicato.com**

<u>Prior Careers and Publications</u>: She was an in-house corporate litigation paralegal for approx. 10 years, and a peaceful contract lawyer for another 10, yet winning any case or court proceeding conducted in Pittsburgh or Key West. Her legal and philosophical publication titles, alone, form a book much, much bigger than this! As also a University Professor, after teaching many things in many places, and winning 2 "Outstanding Professor of the Year" awards at PITT, she retired both careers "until further notice" and took a huge leap of faith, freed herself and followed her own true destiny!